I0140795

SKIN

select poems

by

Nataša Sardžoska

inner child press, ltd.

Credits

Author

Nataša Sardžoska

Editor

hülya n. yılmaz, Ph.D.

Cover Photograph

Hani Arbid

Cover Design

William S. Peters Sr.

inner child press, ltd.

Disclaimer from the Editing Department

Editing is not the exact science one would expect. Many times when considering and employing the rules of English upon a translated work, the authenticity of the authors' words and meaning can be lost. This outcome does not only apply to translations, but also to the writings with a dialectal, colloquial or eclectic style. Sometimes this loss can be profound and deprive the reader of the genuine aspects of the writers' thoughts, feelings and innate flavor. At Inner Child Press International, we strive to maintain the integrity of each and every author's offerings to include seemingly-awkward expressions of those whose native language is not of our own.

General Information

Skin
Nataša Sardžoska

1st Edition: 2019

Publisher Information:
Inner Child Press International
www.innerchildpress.com

ISBN-13 : 978-1-970020-85-4 (inner child press, ltd.)

$ 15.95

I open my soul as a pore
to inhale the light from your eyes,
from your breath.
The heavy day . . .
lost in the torrid arcades of purple-red flesh.

Table of Contents

The Poetry

*T*able of *C*ontents . . . *continued*

*P*hoto *G*allery   29

*E*pilogue   45

Preface

There is a space within me. A space which is homeless. Borderless. A space which is mute. A cellular space. A conflicted space. It overwhelms me. It obsesses me. It disturbs me. It disrupts me. A space that I cannot hear, but I can feel it. The cells are impregnated with memory that I cannot tell. I write poetry to tell. I write to give meaning to those spasmodic voids. I write to interconnect those spaces in my mind. The process is subtle. I cut off the detail, the microscopic fragment, the zero level of the knowing, and I float. I shift in-between words. I reveal the subliminal drift. The tectonic motion of the word.

The chamber character of my poetry reflects that space with which I have communicated in a distinguished fashion. But that space has no words. I had no words when experiencing that space. That space is absorbing spatial memory which is speechless. I give mouth and tongue to that space within my verses and that is the distorted, the bewildered, the unprecedented, the allusive experience. The poems I create become agents of traces that I have accumulated with my sense and sensations. A hotel room, an airport gate, a lobby, a train station, a deserted port, a marine bay, ground control, border crossing, empty restaurants, an old-school bar, crowded streets, massive cities. A silenced space of corporal and sentimental memory.

There is nothing else I can do when I face the white page. I want to see myself inside. I want to tell the world to the world. I want to see. The white page is a mirror. I cannot lie. I cannot hide. I walk on the cadmium textile. I would not be able to write if I was not honest and sincere in my relation to that whiteness, to what I write. I write to calm my nerves. My mood shifts. My despairs . . . My desires . . . I write to fill in the abysses. I write to suffocate my abysses above which I levitate. I defy gravity. I write to save myself from choking. From burning out. From drowning. Writing poetry gives direction to my nervous contortion. In extreme conditions, I often feel the urgent need to write as if there would be some emotional Hiroshima in my inner room if I did not write.

What else can a poet do when (left) alone?
What else when anything else falls apart?
Which space can the poet dwell in?

Yet, I never defined myself as poet, for a poet consists only in the very action of writing. Only in that moment do we give sense to that side of our existence. Outside that moment I execute other everyday dimensions or other dimensions of my ontological being. In the process of poetry-making, I am cutting off the reality to produce another sensational reality. I translate the language. This language can be sometimes obsessive, exuberant, exaggerated or exhilarated, but at other times, it can be mute or even aphasic.

Writing poetry to me is like walking through a tunnel in which I lose myself in the darkness to find myself in the darkness. I face in my poetic experience a lyric subject and I converse with a man, or with you, or with myself. I translate the erotic and the dramatic intercourse in lines of meta-corporal and meta-physical words. I break up with structures. I deconstruct the rhythm. I decompose feelings. I shred answers to the frictions inside myself. I compose images which are terrifying. I capture liminal zones, overheated or frozen moments of space. I close the text, but still, I leave it open. I tackle sensations that are rarely experienced at the end of a poem and I disturb them. I question the word. I analyze the word. I convoke the word. I tie it in a text.

Then, this text becomes a living organism that I need to feed. A living, resurrecting text which proceeds per inner nexus, per consequent analogic illuminations, synthetic aberrations, broken fragments, unreal details, sections, intersections, an interconnectedness without any need or urge to give an explanation or a logical form.

$\mathcal{I}$ write poetry because I do not need to give explanations.

$\mathcal{T}$hose interconnections are implicit even though often rough, spasmodic and cruel for they reveal cellular wounds. Therefore, I need to understand if the word is true or false, and then to enact the word in the nexus. Still, how I feel about it all is very strange: I never re-read what I write. I do not want to experience the same itinerary twice. I do not want to repeat myself.

$\mathcal{T}$he creation is very organic as littoral with broken coasts, stones and bays without any possible road or connection in-between them.

$\mathcal{T}$he meaning sometimes arises in the moment of the creation, and at other times, afterward. It is shifting and slippery yet assertive. It exists in the nostalgia of that space above. It exists in the memory of an accomplished initiation. This is a process of a transfer, or rather a translation, that I really enjoy – of abstract sensations and revelations and of an abstract and ungrammatical language into a palpable, tactile, real, grammatical language. The metaphorical nexus is gnostic, is cognitive: I guide the reader to a journey and an encounter of the process. The purpose is to interconnect and to offer a meaning to the reader, or together with the reader, to myself.

$\mathcal{T}$he selected poems[1] expose inner pain, draw on spiritual freshness, play with the body, depict the organs, build upon tactile brutality, push forward the emotional, reflect oddity and intertwine sensuality and reminiscence of the flesh. Their poetic memory arises from an acute traumatic intercourse, with a somewhat performative character, disarming the horror in this world, capturing the extreme dramaturgy inside the chamber space of the human existence.

---

[1] From the poetry books *Blue Room (*1999*)*, *Skin* (2013), *He Pulled Me with Invisible Strings* (2014), *Living Water* (2016), published in Macedonia, and *Pelle* (2017), published in Italy.

SKIN

select poems

by

Nataša Sardžoska

Skin

Yellow leaves on your skin
Pulled pores of some impalpable silence
Cracked lips
And a fervid valley of thoughts and nipples
Liquid, I say, are you alone
Or does time flow away standing still pretty distant
From the conventional clock?
But I hear on pale layers drops slipping out
Secretion, tears, wine
Yet, it is not the first time nor is it once
But nonce, a perpetual returning back
As you close your eyes facing the choice you do not want to make
As this time comes by, this autumn
On your skin
In an eruption of inconvenient improper indecent spaces

The Tree of Winter

A cold fire in the forest
Rough layers on the edge of this window
I see
I burst shivering without thinking
In a burning interzone
That restores me and glows and wriggles my bones my womb
And yelps without my name without your recognition
A fish from a northern sea
You give me
A grasp of wheat and you spit a bit of wine into my mouth
You are my race, my unease
Turgid seeds
Uprooted dry layers
Your
Skin
On my feet

Nataša Sardžoska

You Are Everywhere

I tear you up
I break apart

papers lost notes with coffee marks bills sugar bags subway tickets
boarding cards stained with wine blue jeans colors notebooks
bus tickets business cards with lipstick marks hidden messages laces
momentums napkins from restaurants strings words in hotel rooms

where nobody goes
I go
I unwind them, they fly
and I deliver myself free to you
I come back to you
without having anything to say

Diamonds

You and I
two endless silences in the sea
two hands that never touch each other but reach out

we walk through the steppes of this city
bewildered by the disobedience in this world
we reap the intense spark from within

to find each other
to clean all the stains inside
to slaughter the worlds in one breath
to grind the precious drops on our bodies

You and I
two endless silences in the sea
two hands that never touch each other but reach out

Liquid Fire

eye to eye, we flow
our bones
broken by the thunderous light of our impossible love . . .
but love is always love
even when the morning is uncertain
even when it is destroying us as a whole
even though we float in the ether of our flesh, our treat
drums beating in our chest shed the burden
leaking out of the space in the morning glory
lonely, I flow into you
confluent of the mute love
bright and serene with the eyes of a child
immaculate and irreversible
a fugitive from the alphabet
a fugitive from mathematics
non-spatial and non-temporal
you and I – two symphonies of a raucous mutism

A Sailing Earthquake

I have revealed the layers
Those unfaithful residues of the cowardly burden
I was born again from silk and blood
I vomited on to the red carpet your nebulous crap
Insidious lies over corrupted surfaces
Those spasmodic sparks of invisible despair
Dimmed lights on the screen
Your face, illuminated,
Searching for my fertile field
I am swollen
Wheat-grain-blown
With an open throat and dislodged ribs
I give myself to you
I dig into the time a crystal sculpture
And everything around is shaking
The earth is boiling
The sea is shivering
The shutters scream
The iron whimpers
Glasses are splashed around
The earthquake has ceased when we met
I gave myself to your ground
I secretly enter with you within, wet . . .

Your body cries of timelessness
Your bones are the spirit of the bed
Your flesh is the space for freedom

Nataša Sardžoska

A Doll on Strings

Walking down the blacktop
while wild rabbits are screaming in boiling water
slaughtered conspiracies
unrevealed words
at each step I take, I inhale blood to live
I am lying down in the gush of bewildered flowers flowing in my hair
You and I,
incalculable steps of the flesh
a city like any other city where we walked
and we did not know
and we did not know each other
when all those energies were fermenting but alive in high water
from the tongues of dead kites to tell us to tell you
I am here
I follow you from each airport gate
I know when I hear your name
it is music with an unknown rhythm
and I tremble from your gaze
and I lost my voice when you came to me
and my skin was becoming darker after each bewildered step of yours
my growing nipples, my lips, burning in winter:
I knew we were the same city
the same shadow
the same rain
and the night before I met you, I was crying like a child
in me, I could hear the screaming of all the slaughtered animals
and I was growing shamelessly mute
wide open legs underneath you
a layer of fertile wheat in your overwhelming whispers
humbly perverse, you arise above the eradicated palls of purple passion

The Limb

A chessboard
our bed
our story
fading away in the distance
echoing through the waves of hotels
we crawl and grope around

Every word is a step
and every step is measured as a word . . .

each cup, a voice of fear
the loneliness, a rhythm embroidered with the wind
written with the promises of the sea's horizon
of the woman bent over a window, smoking and drinking
a glass of the sunset
in the stone fireplace
on the stone of our wild hearts
and even this melody is not enough to sing your sorrow
that blue indigo, desperately breathing in your gaze
calling on the silences of the mute sea
knitting shouts of flames
remote, cloudy, deafening

Every word is a step
and every step is measured as a word . . .

neither one ahead
nor four back

you do not move
I stand in place
it is all in vain

time futilely wasted in missteps
bodies consumed in spirals and swirls

your vulture-hand, a predator rising in the dawn of the space before us

Please go! I say, in the interspace of checkmate

Cortazar's House

Tongues of black wild orchids are thrusting from the subway
When I go out, I behold nothing in my hand but I know where I go
Wild people with weaved hair stop me on their way
The tenth arrondissement is screaming an express boiling pot
Of culinary meat
Breath is becoming thicker as I walk to you alone
While I step down from the fall of someone's else bravery
Cigarettes, stuck on the paving stone
Mute souls
The great morning when you wake me up with your hand in my hair
On the wooden floor, you are searching for your socks
Knees, grass, rainbows
I am stepping down from fragile branches
I fill up the glasses until I start to scroll down from within
High heels are grumbling and bonding to the sound of the Bandoneon
Tongues, serpents, dragons, rhinoceroses are blazing in my head
While I am coming into you frightened
I tightly hold in my hand the code of your gateway

Nataša Sardžoska

Sarajevo

A storm of ice and dust flows in our room
Outside I hear fear, losers, someone else's silence, an insidious plot
I am haunted by a troop of wolves at every step I take on frozen stones
But I feel them devotedly and faithfully
I follow and caress them tenderly
Because this is what we are
Bodies, excommunicated from the world
Distant radio frequencies that no longer exist
But still shimmer on highways
Chess, wine, schnapps, a rug and interlaced snowy curves

I give you my body like a pledge
In this city that never knew rage but is rage now
This night
In me
Is the rage
This bed shifted by the water, flowing underneath the bath

They say, yes, the plumber did not come and the pipe is blocked

So, let all the evil tongues get clogged up
And all the dirty throats strangled
On the helm of disparate movements toward me

Red rose leaves, splashed with sperm
Hannah Arendt's book, falling down the white sheet,
Falling down on me, that chamber
Crawling in the black and white-paved hotel

A crime, I almost commit
Windows, breaking through all around my hips
I am ready to become a shooting mark and a bloody heat
And I shall drown in your brutal times of hoofs raging underneath my skirt
And I shall say nothing

I cry
I beg for mercy
I shall pray
To give you mornings filled with bliss
To walk down the snow without leaving a trace
Not to hurt your love . . .
In this night of grace
Give me your eternal dove

Eclipse

Do not go
right there where you are
the sun goes down and it rises too
in this hotel room, the moon has drowned
at every step you take, the curtains fall down
all those trivial stories of *who* and *why* and *when* tear into pieces
yet, our life is here somewhere stuck in a moment
in a morning scent of scrambled eggs
in the dense and intense aroma of coffee
an imprisoned tongue
tenderness in a wardrobe

Do not go
only these whispers remain eternal
the gentle touch of a yearning desire
the fire burning under two skins
tied up in the flesh
hesitations are suspended
the darkness is falling down
the unclear light of your word . . .

If you go
I will no longer be the one you knew nor shall I be yours
the time shall burn out slowly under the iconic lantern of your joy
it shall slowly wear us off and we shall suffer frantically in silence
deploying our angry teeth as frenzied oxen, awaiting to attack

But even then, stay
let us stick together,
even below the bottom line
let us sweat for the truth
even beyond time
hand in hand!

Do not give me away
do not give up
do not leave me
there from where everybody is running away
we shall be One
we shall become a sound of this untiring symphony
never heard before
never known
we shall rise above
we shall crush the trap
we shall be born again and tramp
we shall let love resurrect
beyond the eclipse of our failed encounter

Nataša Sardžoska

Mute Love

We are not One anymore,
yet we were All
and nothing existed outside ourselves,
outside our nutshell.

Now we are mute,
distant and estranged.
We walk along different platforms.
We make our way through the grey vapor of the carriages
with silky skin, transparent and remote shadows and fog.
There is
nothing,
and nothing will remain after the deaf night
and nothing is what we shall hear,
except the crackling of the rails and the coffee machine:
the muteness is nonce.

In front of your livid paleness,
I stand boiling from within.
I scream and I flow.
Through the corridors, I splutter.
Confused faces are melting behind me.
Unmoved, I stand before you.

I gather inside me scraps, lost suitcases, crumbs of bread,
layers of flesh which have lost their flow,
bewildered in the cold desert.
Ordeals of ferocious beasts,
tongues of mute fires . . .

They are nothing but silence and hatred
While humbly we say, "let's get lost".

A Seafront

There is one zone of bounds far away from you,
distant in our precipice,
in ourselves, wasted
where winds are lost,
where roads are confused . . .
the sincere zone of your failure.

Would you be able to sacrifice your fenced space
in order to be able to breathe?

Yet you still smoulder in the transcendental horizons of silence.
You say you think of the future,
yet you have nowhere left to go for lunch
in your simple present tense.

There is one zone where you do not enter,
where you disseminate fear,
where you can hear all those answers
that you seek but you do not want to find.
A Mediterranean zone
where red cliffs make love with livid depths,
bewildered winds break the compass,
white sails rise above wind-blown hair.

You want to determine your direction
and humbly implore to merge your fetters . . .
in liquid red iron,
in vital peaceful oxygen,
in a flourished green dawn,
but you cannot!

There is a zone
that renews you,
that gives you birth again,
that shapes you and calls you
where windmills grind your remote past tense,
where sailing boats knit your future tense
where gulls weave the travelogue of your flight . . .

but you only keep silent stealthily,
you only wait quietly
and you prey.
You refuse to go
far away, above you . . .

Nataša Sardžoska

The Arcane Light

The fan is open
in the bright abyss of your mind
on the sad margin of your childhood.
Can you burn in your loneliness, free and misunderstood,
in those deserted arcades,
in that city lost in the fog,
the fog of your words,
the words that I hate so much that I would even break them up,
breaking up with the past – with the present past?

Disturb me!
Conquest my bodily cells!
Inject me with light!
Shake me!
Become a hostage in my blood!
Loud as silence,
Dizzying as falling in love,
Reap me as wheat!
Raise me as a child!
Be always there,
My twin,
My substitute,
My enemy!

Deceive me!
Teach me how to walk in the dawn of consciousness,
Immaculate and stuck in the spiral of our love!
Spread me as butter!
Splash me as the moon light!
Save me forever in your oblivion!

The Map of your Winds

In a city on a seashore, we flew against the wind.
We found ourselves in a sea that shivers in obsession.
We found ourselves in a sea that sails in many truths,
unexpected gazes pouring down as morning roses,
entangled hands and legs trying to draw wild embraces
through tears and wine,
through salt and peeled-off skin,
a map of your steps above the sky – separated from all earthly impulses,
a wild thought in your mouth.

We found ourselves alone and we were seeking ourselves alone
in the deserted port of our hotel room,
and all languages weaved at the airport gates were not enough to get you.
In a gallop of bewildered storms of horses coming along,
the cobblestone and women imprisoned, trembling in your rhythm,
boats in the deluge of the silver-grey seas in our deaf nights
shifted our perfect melody,
recognized the power of our steps
painfully as it is painful to leave
to become a Human.

Bodily Ether

I open the wind with the key of your wind.
The storm of your silence is roaring outside.
The northern winds of your trembling heart are blowing.

I open a nostril to make a way for your diffraction
while I transform myself into rain to flow on your skin
to push through and disperse myself in the cracks of your pores.

I open the swinging laurels on my lips – those magnetic forces:
our disobedient cycle of love diffused in my chest,
in my chest that hurts from the void where you no longer exist.

Wanderings

I am wandering by the river, trying to drink your silence.
I am swallowed by that odd moment that you do not want to accept,
And the birth is silent (just as the orgasm!)
And the word should not create you
Because the light is you.

I wander, blown up in the bodily shells,
In the words that I cannot find to reach out to you.
Broken and nude, the waves of our flesh caress me,
Vibrations stronger than the subcutaneous.
Being under your skin is the measure of my time,
Flowing in the presence of your absence.

Nataša Sardžoska

Nameless Streets

I have learned the names of all those streets you walked to come to me.
While I searched for you, the bakery-women were laughing at me.
I became a murderer of our remote times.
Everybody felt my perfume, but only I felt yours in me,
And only you were above all the unpredictable.
I was seeking for you in nameless places, in empty bars,
Eating goat cheese and smoked salmon.

Nobody understands you when you are alone.
There is no worse solitude than seeking the one deep in you, engraved.
The pain is only yours – your one of a kind.

It is six o'clock, and the night is deaf.
You see yourself on me.
This city is a predator.

I have bitten the bitter orange and spit the semen.
I wedged my earring in-between your fingers
To be always there even when you'll be gone.

But you . . .
You have saved me.

Returning

All the roads are melting.
The ones I am walking on by
eradicate the grass of your mind.

All the rivers petrify.
The ones I am drifting along . . .
the silver scepter of your flesh.

Bounding wings in the whirlwind of a suffocated flight,
thunderstruck and thorny,
nests and nets
built around your heart,
used and abused past tenses not existing in any grammar,
verbs of your motion unknown for any law of the physics . . .

False leftovers are breaking down,
vestiges of someone's household.
They fall on you whirring,
abysmal ties in nodes of junctions,
incorporated measures of your lies unknown for any love.

Fragile and exhausted you are, whispering, not knowing how to escape
from the distance between you and your inner self.

There's no love without freedom nor justice nor truth.

Yet you still want to be a child in the sand
as in the back, beyond your childhood
in your native land long time ago,
but there you are, laughing now,
trampling on me . . . broken under your unfair scream.

Nataša Sardžoska

A Strange Bird

You filled my mouth with solemn words,
drowned in blurred whispering waters,
dark and grey – bewildered, untouchable.

You took me to a place that nobody knows,
an always new, always different you,
one step above the whirl – one breath above the wind.

You showed me sandy beaches in winter.
In unreachable peaks of silence have you discovered me.
In this elegant silence have you slaughtered my fears.

You brought me to this nameless city,
rolled me up around myself.
You tied my bones in all four corners of the world
and you pulled them out of my throat to prevent me from choking.

You poured me in your glass to drink me ferociously,
dressed me up in a purple dress
and tied me up around your hair,
your perpetual Bedouin-crown.

I Am Breathing

A heavy overcoat of broken glass,
secret songs of drunk lovers.
Your steps are invisible in the snow,
your body reflections are revealed in the glass.
We are strangers, yet we tremble
in the game of our betrayal.

I open my soul as a pore to inhale the light,
the light from your eyes,
from your breath.
The heavy day is lost in the torrid arcades of purple-red flesh
beneath a sky that no longer exists.

I finish my glass of wine.
Eyes wide shut; I leave traces of lipstick on the crystal.
I swallow you outside the window.
I sow you in hidden streets.
I feel you in my high-heels
in the trumpet of the elevator
in a city that no longer exists.
Alone
with you,
I am breathing.

Photo Gallery

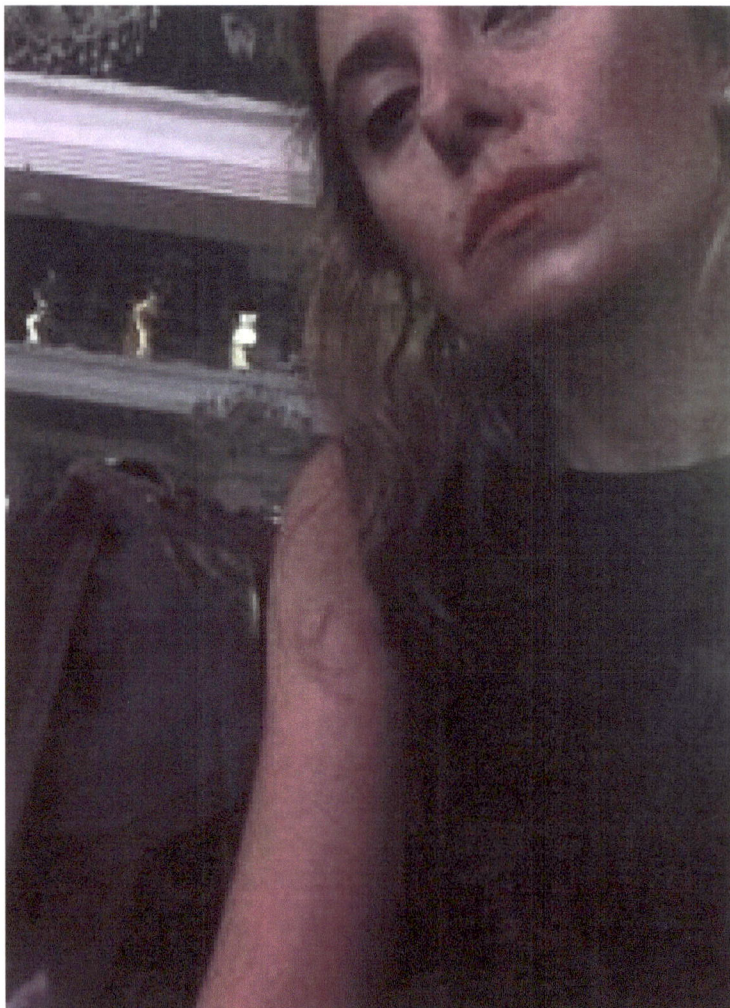

Epilogue

about the *A*uthor . . .

Nataša Sardžoska, Macedonian poet, essayist, writer, literary translator and interpreter (FR, IT, ES, EN, PT, HR, CA), event manager, anthropologist and researcher was born in Skopje in Macedonia on 16.11.1979. She has lived and created her art in many European cities, including Milan, Lisbon, Paris, Brussels and Stuttgart. She holds a Ph.D. in Anthropology from the Eberhard Karls University of Tübingen, Sorbonne Nouvelle in Paris and University of Bergamo, having worked on exiled artists from the former Yugoslavian war, among which David Albahari, Slavenka Drakulic and Tanja Ostojic comprise a few. She is currently an Affiliated Researcher at the Center for Advanced Studies of South East Europe in Rijeka, Croatia and an Assistant professor at the Institute for Anthropology and Ethnology at the Ss. Cyril and Methodious University in Skopje, Macedonia. For her academic work, she collaborates with Radio Koper in Slovenia. She has taught at the Schiller International University in Heidelberg and at the South East European University, Max Van Der Stoel.

*T*he author has published several books of poetry, *Blue Room*, *Skin*, *He Pulled Me with Invisible Strings*, *Living Water* and *Pelle*. Her most recent publication is titled *COCCYX*. Her writings include short stories, essays, critical texts and academic papers. She has been nominated twice for the National Award for best poetry book for her *Brothers Miladinov* at the International Struga Poetry Festival in Macedonia. Her poems have appeared in numerous anthologies. Her poetic work has been translated into Serbian, Italian, Spanish, Slovakian, German, Croatian and English, some of which have been published in literary reviews, such as *Buenos Aires Poetry*, *Hablemos Claro* in Honduras, *Circulo de Poesia* in Mexico, *Strane* in Bosnia, *Polja* in Serbia and *Argo* in Italy. She has written reviews for *Doppiozero* and *Nuova Prosa* in Milan, *Blesok* in Skopje and *Transmidia* in Rio de Janeiro. She has translated from Italian, Portuguese and Catalan the following writers: Pasolini, Carducci, Luzi, Saba, Montale, Quasimodo, Sanguineti, Merini, Ortese, Levi, Zanzotto, Fortini, Bertolucci, Saramago, Pessoa, Camoes, Braga, Carvalho, Amaral, Bojunga, Tabucchi, Bufalino, Petroni, Carneiro,

Correia, Tavares, Tozzi, Couto, Cruz, Baricco, Benni, Moraes, Moreira, Fazzini, Fratus, Guimaraes and Pedrals. In 2002, she has won a prize from the Ministry of Foreign Affairs of Italy for best first translation in Macedonian language of *Pinocchio*, a book by Carlo Collodi.

Nataša Sardžoska's poetry readings are recitals with performative and interactive character: She combines vocal experiments, music, improvisation, body-paint and dance, and she interacts with the audience each time in a different way. She has performed her poetry at the Ars Poetica Festival in Bratislava singing an authentic Macedonian song. During her poetry reading on the Versopolis-platform at the International Poetry Festival in Genova, she has performed a-cappella together with the French jazz singer, Charlène Puyguiraud and body-paint with the Italian artist Cosimo Frezzolini. At the Modoars Festival for Contemporary Music, the author has performed her poems together with Milica Dobaj (soprano, Montenegro), Rosalba Colosimo (soprano, Italy) and with Ema Popivoda (piano, Macedonia) inviting the audience to write on her skin. She had a poetry reading at the Literary Festival Scream in Rijeka and interpreted poems by Rade Serbedzija at the Museum Revoltella in Trieste. She has collaborated with the French Institute and the French Embassy in Skopje organizing the poetic soirée, Les rivages de l'exil for Francophone poetry on exile and the Soirée aux jardins. In collaboration with the Italian Embassy in Skopje, which organized an Italian poetic-musical evening, Il vino è la poesia della terra, she has performed poems in Italian. She has presented her performative art and her poetry also during her visit to the Macedonian Cultural Center in Sofia. At the Academy of Arts in Berlin, together with the Macedonian guitarist and composer, Georgi Sareski, she performed her poetry-musical recital barefoot in a unique dance performance for the Poetry Festival of Berlin. Her poem, "Doll on Strings", has been published in English and Spanish in the International Poetry Anthology Against Child Abuse. She has attended the Sha'ar International Poetry Festival in Tel Aviv, where she performed with sax, contrabass and contemporary dances in a poetry, dance and music improvisation event.

The author has founded the Argentine Tango Association in Macedonia in 2008, and has been promoting Argentinian poetry, music and dance ever since.

Nataša Sardžoska's poetry intertwines sensuality, the reminiscence of the flesh, exposes inner pain and reveals a spiritual freshness. Her poetic memory has performative character, capturing the dramaturgy of the chamber-space of the human existence.

Reviews & Critiques

Nataša Sardžoska and her book of poetry,
He Pulled Me with Invisible Strings

Occupy Poetry: The Punch and Judy Show in Nataša Sardžoska's book of poetry, *He Pulled Me with Invisible Strings*

After publishing her books of poetry, *Blue Room* (Dialog, Skopje, 1999), *Skin* (De Odorico Casa, Skopje, 2013), *He Pulled Me with Invisible Strings* (Poetiki, Skopje, 2014), Nataša Sardžoska was nominated for the national award of the best book of the year for her *Brothers Miladinov* and *Living Water* (Makavej, 2017) at the International Festival of Poetry in Struga. Her book, *Pelle*, has appeared in its Italian translation on "Versopolis", an EU-literary platform

The titles of all books by the author are highly allusive and impetuous in their allusiveness. The space of poetic interest is dramatized and focuses on Eros. Her writings focus, in fact, on the conversion of *eros* to *thanatos*, and then, in a deeper phase, are transformed into a memory full of sensual vibrations and syncretism. From the chamber environment of the *Blue Room* that which with one eye looks toward the blue sky (the blue sea, the blue spirit) through the human environment and the shadow of the corporal complexion (skin, flesh) in that room, Nataša Sardžoska moves on to the dramaturgical aspects of the human being's chamber space. The drama of human existence (the existential and phenomenological frame) best reflects the complex of the human being (the essential and ontological forms), and through this, the traumatic drama of the Being of the world.

In her third collection of poetry, the author captures the dramaturgy of the chamber space of human existence through allusions to the puppet theater. In fact, *He Pulled Me with Invisible Strings* is a poetic performance of a marionette, or a monodrama of puppets and marionettes in poetic form – from where the book's title originates. Hence, the performative character of poetic memory. Hence, the exaggerated sensibility of flash-reminiscences. Hence, the pathos of addressing the Other. Hence, the interlocutor's implicity, the speaker's explicitness – the speaker as in the lyrical subject, the creator of the drama and the monologue. Hence, the discretion of the tribute or the unsuspected dedication to Homme – Man. Hence, the dialogic strategy of the word, of the discourse that recalls, that remembers: because behind the word lies an excited and perturbing consciousness, a being that tends to surpass the fence and the temporal barriers, to transcend the frontiers between the real and the fictitious, to transform the past into the present, to transpose the experience in the body into the hedonism of the text. Hence, the transmutation of nostalgia for the voluptuous into the occupation of poetry: Occupy Poetry!

Why do I read the author's third book through the prism of the appealing concept of conquering poetry, occupying poetry?

In *He Pulled Me with Invisible Strings*, the threads of the narration are intertwined in the complexity of the poetic structure (enunciation, meaning, style) with their descriptive inversions – with the inversion of epithets, attributes, nouns and verbs, settings of space, both the micro-space of the body / two bodies in one, and the broader one – a room, a hotel room, a hotel lobby, an airport, gates, a railway station, a train, a beach, a marine bay, the littoral . . . For this reason, the nomadic vocation of the subject is experienced as linguistic nomadism, whereas poetry is performed as nomadic poetry. This nomadic poetry is sculpted and resistant to temporal, spatial, racial, linguistic, cultural and existential dislocations. It is hybrid. It is bipolar poetry. In the poems, the voice of the subject is in panic, except that it is a voice that repeats the enjoyment and pleasure of another time, of a past that lives, and in fact, is no longer a past. It is here, it is in us; so, it exists. We are the nomadic poetry.

The utterances in Nataša Sardžoska's poetry involve a changeable rhythm which is fast, quick, brief, ecstatic sometimes, and at other times, slow – slow as if trying to postpone the end, to keep the event active, the intimate event. The act of recognition, of mutual identification of one in the other, is the absolute act. There are no doubts either of the dilemmas in this act. There is no room for skepticism, for doubt, for hesitations. This act is concluded and complete, and there is no room for anything else. Life and reality are anything but different things, partially, fragmentarily, incomplete, inhibited, cut off from their integrity. There are other reasons why a poet can imagine both when s/he reflects on the future and when s/he remembers the past.

In the collection, *He Pulled Me with Invisible Strings* one senses an almost pathetic tension between the word and the thought, between the corporal and the spiritual, between being and being. In poems of this genre – allusive, personal and intimate to the point of reaching pain, confessional to the extent of terror, there reigns a reasoning to be understood as a harness, a harness of speech and thought, of flesh and feeling, of bodily and psychic sensations. This book constitutes a subjective form of lyric poetry; however, we recognize the echoing of an archetype (the universal matrix) throughout. This is the archetype of Animus and Soul, which, in the act of self-identification (self-recognition) in the Other and in the Other within us, are inseparable. The verses are composed to become a shrill cry and a desire for that essential inseparability, like a challenge ritual, or as an act of contradiction toward that reality which is an arena of separations – an arena that systematically produces disabled, marginal, exploited and manipulated subjects, the puppet-like individuals and of the marionettes.

Nataša Sardžoska's work in *He Pulled Me with Invisible Strings* is indicative of contemporary contextualization within Macedonian poetry. This form of poetry returns to the ancient forms and thus evidences that they are eternal. Those are the forms of the intimate lyric, of the confessional lyric, of the supreme lyric, if we want, even sonnet or haiku. Young poets, the contemporary witnesses of the ugly and brutal reality of the beginning of the century (the beginning of the twenty-first century) in Macedonia and in the world, give resistance to the strategies of deprivation and exclusion of the world of soul and spirituality, to the reductive and revisionist strategies that are culturally and politically inclined to the simplification of human civilization with the help of modern technologies. They oppose and reject the reduction of the human being to a puppet, rebelling against the transformation of the world into a global theater of a Punch and Judy Show of marionettes. The very consciousness they represent is already a form of revolt, of rebellion, a new resistance, and thus, it is the seminal nutshell of the new poetics as articulated in Nataša Sardžoska's book, *He Pulled Me with Invisible Strings*: Occupy Poetry!

Katica Kjulavkova
Academic, writer and literary critic
Member, The Academy of Arts and Sciences of Republic of Macedonia

In her third poetry book, *He Pulled Me with Invisible Strings*, the Macedonian poet Nataša Sardžoska, an outstanding translator and interpreter of various languages (Italian, French, Portuguese, Spanish and English) as well as a Ph.D. holder in anthropology and sociology, has introduced to us her own love-world and love-simulacrum, which the title allusively announces. This book is almost an intermedia-nexus between poetry and theatrical play, especially the lyric one – the psycho-drama of what has been endured and felt. In her poems, the author reveals a sincere and fresh language, just as her entire poetic creation is. Sardžoska is a well-established poet, a globetrotter with Apollonian-Dionysian tendencies and an excellent scholar of media, communication and culture.

Ivan Djeparovski
Professor of Philosophy and Aesthetics
at St. Cyril and Methodius University, Macedonia
Writer and literary critic

The untranslatability of Nataša Sardžoska's poetry is terrifying and at the same time unique and powerful. In this book of poetry, there is a palpitation of something raw and definite, something definitely definite, yet something that cannot be further improved upon. Something perfect, authentic and truthful.

Jonathan Pollock
Professor of English Literature at the University of Perpignan, France
Writer and literary critic

There is a lot of passion and freshness here. Exposed inner pain. I would like to find ways to universalize it all more. I guess, I am saying the poet has shred individual responses to horror in the world. But there are also universal images, effects, structures, feelings, touches and attitudes.

Richard Becker
Professor at the University of Richmond, USA
Poet, pianist, composer and chamber musician

I was struck by the sensuality of the flesh, which is perfectly intertwined with the spirituality of her poetry.

Mehmed Begic
Writer and editor

Inner Child Press

Inner Child Press is a publishing company founded and operated by writers. Our personal publishing experiences provide us an intimate understanding of the sometimes-daunting challenges writers, new and seasoned may face in the business of publishing and marketing their creative "Written Work".

For more information:

Inner Child Press

www.innerchildpress.com

intouch@innerchildpress.com

Inner Child Press International

'building bridges of cultural understanding'

202 Wiltree Court, State College, Pennsylvania 16801

www.innerchildpress.com

www.ingramcontent.com/pod-product-compliance
Lightning Source LLC
Chambersburg PA
CBHW041425090426

42741CB00002B/41